Don't Give Up

on

life	ideas	dreams	children	prayers
faith	hope	love	jobs	marriage
family	parents		neighbors	

If **A** ^{and} **B** *doesn't work; you still have* **C** ^{thru} **Z**

to find solutions, don't give up!

(26) x 3 (78) biblical reasons *aligned with each letter of the alphabet* that will:

1. encouraged **2.** produce hope **3.** motivate to keep trying

written by: **Brenda J. Mills**

inspired by: **Destini` J. Stephens**

All Bible Scripture Text:
King James Version
Scripture Highlighted in Red: Jesus is Speaking

All Word Definitions are from:
Thorndike Barnhart, Scott Foresman
Advanced Dictionary, 1997

Printed in the United States of America

Support Team:
Tony L. Mills, Sr., Destini' J. Stephens

Book Cover Design
Brenda J. Mills

Dedication

This book is dedicated to God. For never leaving nor forsaking me. For giving me ears to hear, spiritual eyes to see and a mind to understand.

For allowing a portion of Him to dwell in me, the Holy Spirit. And for giving to the world His Only Begotten Son, Jesus who is the author and finisher of faith and the perfect role model for a person's life.

He watched over me all of my life, even before I ever acknowledged Him, His grace and mercy sustained, protected and carried me. And who reminds me during unquestionable times that, "Many are the afflictions of the righteous but the Lord, (He) will deliver us out of them all." Psalms 34:19 Because, "Every word of God is pure, He is a shield to them who put their trust in Him." Proverbs 30:5

I'm grateful daily, happy and blessed to be saved. Thank you Father God for loving me unconditionally.

Preface

Are you following the Word of God, regarding situations?

Whatever the Word of God says to do (*from reading, a positive thought coming to your mind, through an encouraging word from someone*) regarding your matter, do it. And you will have peace, instructions to accomplish, delivered and made free. No more delays, defeats, discouragements and defects, victories only!

Also, some of the scriptures may need to be read more than once, *"The words of the LORD are pure words: as silver tried in a furnace of earth, purified seven times."* ^{Psalms 12:6} but have faith, keeping reading and doing as your directed for the better and best results.

Why settle, if not A then B. And if A nor B worked, you still have 24 additional ways left (C-Z). Remember: (26) Ways (78) Reasons Don't Give Up.

Introduction

The Word of God (the bible) works! All words do what they are supposed to do. A person can say something and make someone feel good or feel bad. Someone can also say something and have a positive or negative effect. (26) Ways (78) Reasons Don't Give Up, are biblical words that pertain to various issues. The pages are alphabetically positioned with words that began with the particular letter of the alphabet aligned with scriptures. Why, because that's how the idea to write this book came about.

I was at my daughter's home during the weekend of her daughters' senior open house. And Des seemed to be somewhat puzzled as she was trying to figure out which task to tackle with first from the list her mom had texted to her. And me trying to encourage her said, if **A** doesn't work out try **B** and if it doesn't work, keep trying you have twenty-six ways (26). And Des with excitement, immediately said where is that in the Bible, and boom I knew I had to write a book pertaining to that communicating moment.

This book has (26) x 3 = (78) biblical defined words and scriptures to: encourage, heal, create hope, get a breakthrough, locate answers, receive confirmation and become free, regarding various situations that pertains to the issues of life. I don't know personally how the Lord is going to interact with you while reading this book, but be assured he will. *"Draw nigh to God, and he will draw nigh to you."* *James 4:8* And that's done by reading his Word, He is the Word. *"In the beginning was the Word, and the Word was with God, and the Word was God."* *John 1:1*

A – One (1)

Ask: try to find out by words; inquire. Seek the answer to. Put a question to; inquire of. Try to get by words.

Avoid: keep away: We avoided large cities on our trip. Have Nothing to do with. Make void; annul.

Awake: come out of sleep; wake up; arouse. Bestir (make a mental or physical effort), rouse oneself; become vigilant. Awake to, become aware of; realize.

- **Ask**, and it shall be given you; seek, and ye shall find; knock, and it shall be opened unto you: For every one that **asketh** receiveth; and he that seeketh findeth; and to him that knocketh it shall be opened. Or what man is there of you, whom if his son **ask** bread, will he give him a stone? Or if he **ask** a fish, will he give him a serpent? If ye then, being evil, know how to give good gifts unto your children, how much more shall your Father which is in heaven give good things to them that **ask** him? Therefore all things whatsoever ye would that men should do to you, do ye even so to them: for this is the law and the prophets. Matthew 7:7-12

- Study to shew thyself approved unto God, a workman that needeth not to be ashamed, rightly dividing the word of truth. But **shun (avoid)** profane *and* vain babblings: for they will increase unto more ungodliness. 2 Timothy 2:15-16

- Flee also youthful lusts: but follow righteousness, faith, charity, peace, with them that call on the Lord out of a pure heart. But foolish and unlearned questions **avoid**, knowing that they do gender strife. And the servant of the Lord must not strive; but be gentle unto all *men*, apt to teach, patient, In meekness instructing those that oppose themselves; if God peradventure will give them repentance to the acknowledging of the truth; And *that* they may recover themselves out of the snare of the devil, who are taken captive by him at his will. 2 Timothy 2:22-26

- **Awake** to righteousness, and sin not; for some have not the knowledge of God: I speak this to your shame. 1 Corinthians 15:34

2

Have you humbled yourself and
<u>asked</u> someone to help you… it's okay

B - Two (2)

Battle: a hostile engagement or encounter between opposing armies, air forces, or navies; combat; fight. A fight between two persons; single combat; duel. Actual hostilities between nations; fight or warfare. Any struggle for victory; conflict; contest. Strive for victory; struggle; contend.

Believe: accept as true or real. Think somebody tells the truth. Think; suppose. Have faith (in a person or thing); trust.

Blessed: holy, sacred. Bringing joy; joyful. Happy; fortunate enjoying the favor of heaven; beatified.

- I returned, and saw under the sun, that the race is not to the swift, nor the **battle** to the strong, neither yet bread to the wise, nor yet riches to men of understanding, nor yet favour to men of skill; but time and chance happeneth to them all. Ecclesiastes 9:11

- Let not your heart be troubled: ye **believe** in God, believe also in me. In my Father's house are many mansions: if it were not so, I would have told you. I go to prepare a place for you. And if I go and prepare a place for you, I will come again, and receive you unto myself; that where I am, there ye may be also. And whither I go ye know, and the way ye know. Thomas saith unto him, LORD, we know not whither thou goest; and how can we know the way? Jesus saith unto him, I am the way, the truth, and the life: no man cometh unto the Father, but by me. If ye had known me, ye should have known my Father also: and from henceforth ye know him, and have seen him. John 14:1-7

- Jesus said unto him, If thou canst **believe**, all things are possible to him that believeth. Mark 9:23

- **Blessed** are the peacemakers: for they shall be called the children of God. Matthew 5:9

Your every concern and answer, is in the Word of God, the <u>Bible</u>.

C - Three (3)

Commit: do or perform (usually something wrong). Hand over for safekeeping; deliver.   Give over; carry over; transfer. Involve.

Confess: own up to; acknowledge; admit. Tell (one's sins) to a priest in order to obtain forgiveness. Acknowledge or admit to a crime, fault, etc.

Counsellors: person who gives advice; adviser. Lawyer. Instructor or leader in a summer camp.

- **Commit** thy way unto the LORD; trust also in him; and he shall bring it to pass. <u>Psalm 37:5</u>

- **Confess** your faults one to another, and pray one for another, that ye may be healed. The effectual fervent prayer of a righteous man availeth much. <u>James 5:16</u>

- Where no counsel is, the people fall: but in the multitude of **counsellors** there is safety. <u>Proverbs 11:14</u>

<u>Cast</u> your every care upon God, His Word, His ways, His instructions.

D - Four (4)

Decree: something ordered or settled by authority; official decision. A decision or order of a court or judge. A law of a church council, especially one settling a disputed point of doctrine. Order or settle by authority. Decide; determine.

Delight: great pleasure; joy. something which gives great pleasure. Please greatly. Have great pleasure.

Desire: a wanting or longing. Strong wish: a desire to travel. Thing wished for. Express a wish for; ask for.

Doubt Not: not believe or trust; not be sure of; feel uncertain about: I doubt that he wrote the letter. Be uncertain or undecided. Difficulty in believing.

- Thou shalt also **decree** a thing, and it shall be established unto thee: and the light shall shine upon thy ways. <u>Job 22:28</u>

- **Delight** thyself also in the LORD: and he shall give thee the **desires** of thine heart. <u>Psalm 37:4</u>

- Now in the morning as he returned into the city, he hungered. And when he saw a fig tree in the way, he came to it, and found nothing thereon, but leaves only, and said unto it, Let no fruit grow on thee henceforward for ever. And presently the fig tree withered away. And when the disciples saw it, they marvelled, saying, How soon is the fig tree withered away! Jesus answered and said unto them, Verily I say unto you, If ye have faith, and **doubt not**, ye shall not only do this which is done to the fig tree, but also if ye shall say unto this mountain, Be thou removed, and be thou cast into the sea; it shall be done. And all things, whatsoever ye shall ask in prayer, believing, ye shall receive. <u>Matthew 21:18-22</u>

<u>Dare</u> yourself and try doing things God's way for 26 days.

E - Five (5)

Established: set up on a firm or permanent basis: establish a government. Settle in position; set up a business.

Expected: think something will probably come or happen; look forward to. Look forward to with reason or confidence: I shall expect to find that job finished by Saturday. Count on as necessary or right.

Eye: the part of the body by which human beings and animals see; organ of sight. The colored part of the eye; iris. And organ that is sensitive to light. Ability to see small differences in things. Look, glance. A watchful look; careful regard.

- Commit thy works unto the Lord; and thy thoughts shall be **established**. Proverbs 16:3

- For I know the thoughts that I think toward you, saith the LORD, thoughts of peace, and not of evil, to give you an **expected** end. Jeremiah 29:11

- But as it is written, **Eye** hath not seen, nor ear heard, neither have entered into the heart of man, the things which God hath prepared for them that love him. But God hath revealed them unto us by his Spirit: for the Spirit searcheth all things, yea, the deep things of God. 1 Corinthians 2:9-10

Encourage and challenge yourself
sometimes.

F – Six (6)

Faith: belief without proof; trust: We have faith in our friends. Belief in God, religion, or spiritual things. What is believed; doctrine or tenet.

Favour: act of kindness. Exceptional kindness. Liking; approval: They will look with favor on your plan. Condition of being liked, accepted, or approved.

Find: come upon by chance; happen on; meet with: *He found a dime in the road.* Look for and get. See; know; feel; perceive. Get; get the use of. Arrive at; reach. Decide and declare. Gain or recover the use of. Provide; supply.

- And, behold, a woman, which was diseased with an issue of blood twelve years, came behind him, and touched the hem of his garment: For she said within herself, If I may but touch his garment, I shall be whole. But Jesus turned him about, and when he saw her, he said, Daughter, be of good comfort; thy **faith** hath made thee whole. And the woman was made whole from that hour. <u>Matthew 9:20-22</u>

- Even so **faith**, if it hath not works, is dead, being alone. Yea, a man may say, Thou hast **faith**, and I have works: shew me thy **faith** without thy works, and I will shew thee my **faith** by my works. <u>James 2:17-18</u>

- Whoso loveth instruction loveth knowledge: but he that hateth reproof *is* brutish. A good *man* obtaineth **favour** of the LORD: but a man of wicked devices will he condemn. A man shall not be established by wickedness: but the root of the righteous shall not be moved. <u>Proverbs 12:1-3</u>

- Hear instruction and be wise, And do not disdain *it.* Blessed is the man who listens to me, Watching daily at my gates, Waiting at the posts of my doors. For whoever **finds** me finds life, And obtains favour from the LORD. <u>Proverbs 8:33-35</u>

17

<u>Forget</u> about how you made a mess earlier in the day, or yesterday. Start over and try again, now.

Now never ends.

G – Seven (7)

Give: hand over as a gift; make a present of: *give money to charity*. Hand over: *Give me a pencil*. Hand over in return for something; pay: *she gave $3 for the wagon*. Let have.

God: the Supreme Being worshipped in most religions as the maker and ruler of the world. God, a being that is thought to have supernatural or superhuman powers and considered worthy of worship.

Grace: beauty of form, movement, or manner; pleasing or agreeable quality; charm, ease, or elegance. Goodwill; favor. Mercy or pardon. The favor and love of God: fall from grace. A short prayer of thanks given before or after a meal.

- Give, and it shall be **given** unto you; good measure, pressed down, and shaken together, and running over, shall men **give** into your bosom. For with the same measure that ye mete withal it shall be measured to you again. Luke 6:38

- In the beginning was the Word, and the Word was with **God**, and the Word was **God**. The same was in the beginning with **God**. All things were made by him; and without him was not any thing made that was made. In him was life; and the life was the light of men. And the light shineth in darkness; and the darkness comprehended it not. John 1:1-5

- For the LORD God is a sun and shield: the LORD will give **grace** and glory: no good thing will he withhold from them that walk uprightly. O LORD of hosts, blessed is the man that trusteth in thee. Psalm 84:11-12

- The curse of the LORD is in the house of the wicked: but he blesseth the habitation of the just. Surely he scorneth the scorners: but he giveth **grace** unto the lowly. The wise shall inherit glory: but shame shall be the promotion of fools. Proverbs 3:33-35

Give up trying to do it alone. Ask the Lord to send you help.

H - Eight (8)

Health: a being well; freedom from sickness. Condition of body or mind: *be in excellent health.* Sound condition; well being; welfare: *the safety and health of the whole state.*

Help: provide with what is needed or useful: *help a hospital with one's money. My parents helped me with my homework.* Relieve (a person) in want, trouble, or distress. Assist in bringing about.

Holy Ghost: spirit of God; third person of the Trinity; Holy Spirit, that God has given and allow to dwell within us to help and teach us all things.

- For I will restore **health** unto thee, and I will heal thee of thy wounds, saith the LORD; because they called thee an Outcast, *saying*, This *is* Zion, whom no man seeketh after. <u>Jeremiah 30:17</u>

- God *is* our refuge and strength, a very present **help** in trouble. Therefore will not we fear, though the earth be removed, and though the mountains be carried into the midst of the sea; *Though* the waters thereof roar *and* be troubled, *though* the mountains shake with the swelling thereof. Selah. <u>Psalms 46:1-3</u>

- Jesus answered and said unto him, If a man love me, he will keep my words: and my Father will love him, and we will come unto him, and make our abode with him. He that loveth me not keepeth not my sayings: and the word which ye hear is not mine, but the Father's which sent me. These things have I spoken unto you, being yet present with you. But the **Comforter**, which is the **Holy Ghost**, whom the Father will send in my name, he shall teach you all things, and bring all things to your remembrance, whatsoever I have said unto you. <u>John 14:23-26</u>

- The God of our ancestors raised Jesus from the dead-whom you killed by hanging him on a cross. God exalted him to his own right hand as Prince and Savior that he might bring Israel to repentance and forgive their sins. We are witnesses of these things, and so is the **Holy Spirit**, whom God has given to those who obey him. <u>Acts 5:30-32</u>

23

Throw your <u>hands</u> up in the air and ask the Lord, the Holy Spirit to <u>help</u> you.

I – Nine (9)

Inquire: try to find out by questions; ask. Make a search for information, knowledge, or truth; make an examination of facts or principles. Ask about; try to find out by question.

Inspiration: influence of thought and strong feelings on actions, especially on good actions: *Some people get inspiration from sermons, some from poetry.* Any influence that arouses effort to do well.

Instructions: a teaching or education. Knowledge or teaching given; lesson. Directions; orders.

- "Go, **inquire** of the LORD for me, and for those who are left in Israel and Judah, concerning the words of the book that is found; for great *is* the wrath of the LORD that is poured out on us, because our fathers have not kept the word of the LORD, to do according to all that is written in this book." 2 Chronicles 34:21

- All scripture is given by **inspiration** of God, and is profitable for doctrine, for reproof, for correction, for instruction in righteousness: That the man of God may be perfect, thoroughly furnished unto all good works. 2 Timothy 2:16-17

- Apply thine heart unto **instruction**, and thine ears to the words of knowledge. Proverbs 23:12

<u>Incline</u> thyself to be quiet and hear what someone is saying.

J - Ten (10)

Jesus: founder of the Christian religion. The name means God is salvation. Jesus Christ.

Joy: a strong feeling of pleasure arising from a sense of well-being or satisfaction; gladness; happiness. Something that causes gladness or happiness: *On a hot day, a cool; swim is a joy.*

Just: no more than; only; merely: *We are just an ordinary family, neither rich nor poor.* Barley; quite; truly positively. Exactly. Almost exactly. In accordance with what is right and honest; fair: a just price. Deserved; merited; due: a just reward. Having good grounds; well-founded. True; correct; exact: a just description. In accordance with standards or requirements; proper: just proportions. Righteous; upright: a just life. Lawful.

- Now the birth of **Jesus Christ** was on this wise: When as his mother Mary was espoused to Joseph, before they came together, she was found with child of the Holy Ghost. Then Joseph her husband, being a just man, and not willing to make her a public example, was minded to put her away privily. But while he thought on these things, behold, the angel of the LORD appeared unto him in a dream, saying, Joseph, thou son of David, fear not to take unto thee Mary thy wife: for that which is conceived in her is of the Holy Ghost. And she shall bring forth a son, and thou shalt call his name **Jesus**: for he shall save his people from their sins. <u>Matthew 1:18-21</u>

- Then said they unto him, LORD, evermore give us this bread. And **Jesus** said unto them, I am the bread of life: he that cometh to me shall never hunger; and he that believeth on me shall never thirst. <u>John 6:34-35</u>

- Create in me a clean heart, O God; and renew a right spirit within me. Cast me not away from thy presence; and take not thy holy spirit from me. Restore unto me the **joy** of thy salvation; and uphold me *with thy* free spirit. *Then* will I teach transgressors thy ways; and sinners shall be converted unto thee. <u>Psalms 51:10-13</u>

- The **just** *man* walketh in his integrity: his children *are* blessed after him. <u>Proverbs 20:7</u>

Call on the majestic <u>Name of Jesus,</u> anytime, anywhere and any place.

K - Eleven (11)

Keep: have for a long time or forever: *you may keep this book*. Have and not let go: keep a secret. Have and take care of.

Keys: a small metal instrument for locking and unlocking the lock of a door. A padlock. Anything shaped or used like it: a roller-skate key. The answer to a puzzle or problem. Sheet or book of answers: *a key to a test*.

Kind: doing good rather than harm; friendly: a kind girl. Gentle: be kind to animals. Showing or characterized by kindness: kind words. Gracious mean having or showing a generous, sympathetic, considerate attitude toward others. Kind implies that the attitude is genuine, natural, and sincere.

- Ye shall therefore **keep** my statutes, and my judgments: which if a man do, he shall live in them: I *am* the LORD.
Leviticus 18:5

- When Jesus came into the coasts of Caesarea Philippi, he asked his disciples, saying, Whom do men say that I the Son of man am? And they said, Some say that thou art John the Baptist: some, Elias; and others, Jeremias, or one of the prophets. He saith unto them, But whom say ye that I am? And Simon Peter answered and said, Thou art the Christ, the Son of the living God. And Jesus answered and said unto him, Blessed art thou, Simon Barjona: for flesh and blood hath not revealed it unto thee, but my Father which is in heaven. And I say also unto thee, That thou art Peter, and upon this rock I will build my church; and the gates of hell shall not prevail against it. And I will give unto thee the **keys** of the kingdom of heaven: and whatsoever thou shalt bind on earth shall be bound in heaven: and whatsoever thou shalt loose on earth shall be loosed in heaven. Then charged he his disciples that they should tell no man that he was Jesus the Christ.
Matthew 16:13-20

- Put on therefore, as the elect of God, holy and beloved, bowels of mercies, **kindness**, humbleness of mind, meekness, longsuffering; Forbearing one another, and forgiving one another, if any man have a quarrel against any: even as Christ forgave you, so also *do* ye.
Colossians 3:12-13

Keep trying, keep believing and trusting, God.

L - Twelve (12)

Lack: be without; have not: *A homeless person lacks a home.* Have not enough. Fact or condition of being without. Not having enough of something, good or bad. Shortage. Thing needed. Want means to lack something worth have, desired, or especially, necessary for completeness.

Lord: One who has power over others or to whom service and obedience are due; master, ruler, or chief. The Lord, a God. Christ (in Great Britain) a man of rank; peer of the realm; person entitle by courtesy to the title of lord.

Love: a warm and tender liking; deep feeling of fondness and friendship; great affection or devotion: love of one's family, love for a friend. A strong or passionate affection for a person one desires sexually.

- And he said unto them, When I sent you without purse, and scrip, and shoes, <u>lacked</u> ye any thing? And they said, Nothing. Then said he unto them, But now, he that hath a purse, let him take *it*, and likewise *his* scrip: and he that hath no sword, let him sell his garment, and buy one. <u>Luke 22:35</u>

- The <u>LORD</u> *is* the portion of mine inheritance and of my cup: thou maintainest my lot. <u>Psalms 16:5</u>

- Ye have heard that it hath been said, Thou shalt love thy neighbour, and hate thine enemy. But I say unto you, <u>Love</u> your enemies, bless them that curse you, do good to them that hate you, and pray for them which despitefully use you, and persecute you; That ye may be the children of your Father which is in heaven: for he maketh his sun to rise on the evil and on the good, and sendeth rain on the just and on the unjust. For if ye <u>love</u> them which <u>love</u> you, what reward have ye? do not even the publicans the same? And if ye salute your brethren only, what do ye more than others? do not even the publicans so? Be ye therefore perfect, even as your Father which is in heaven is perfect. <u>Matthew 5:43-48</u>

Listen.

M – Thirteen (13)

Man: an adult male person. A human being; person; individual: No man can be sure of the future. All men are created equal. All human beings; the human race.

Mercy: more kindness than justice requires; kindness beyond what can be claimed or expected. Kindly treatment; pity: deeds of mercy. Something to be thankful for. Blessing: *It's a mercy that you weren't injured in the accident.*

Mountain: a very high hill; a natural elevation of the earth's surface rising high above the surrounding level. A very large heap or pile of anything: a mountain of rubbish. A huge amount: amount of difficulties.

- Then was Jesus led up of the Spirit into the wilderness to be tempted of the devil. And when he had fasted forty days and forty nights, he was afterward an hungered. And when the tempter came to him, he said, If thou be the Son of God, command that these stones be made bread. But he answered and said, It is written, **Man** shall not live by bread alone, but by every word that proceedeth out of the mouth of God. Matthew 4:2-4

- But God, who is rich in **mercy**, for his great love wherewith he loved us, Even when we were dead in sins, hath quickened us together with Christ, (by grace ye are saved;) And hath raised us up together, and made us sit together in heavenly places in Christ Jesus: That in the ages to come he might shew the exceeding riches of his grace in his kindness toward us through Christ Jesus. For by grace are ye saved through faith; and that not of yourselves: it is the gift of God: Not of works, lest any man should boast. For we are his workmanship, created in Christ Jesus unto good works, which God hath before ordained that we should walk in them. Ephesians 2:4-10

- Even them will I bring to my holy **mountain**, and make them joyful in my house of prayer: their burnt offerings and their sacrifices *shall be* accepted upon mine altar; for mine house shall be called an house of prayer for all people. Isaiah 56:7

<u>Make</u> a joyful noise unto the Lord, in your atmosphere, right where you are, now.

N – Fourteen (14)

Neglect: give too little care or attention to; slight: neglect one's health. Leave undone; not attend to: *The man neglected her work.* Omit; fail. Act or fact of neglecting; disregard. Want of attention to what should be done.

Never: not ever; at no time: *He never has seen a more perfect copy.* In no case; not at all; to not extent or degree. Never so, a not even so. No matter how.

Nourish: make grow, or keep alive and well, with food; feed; nurture: *Milk nourishes a baby.* Maintain, foster, or support: nourish a hope. Nourishing: *keeping well-fed and healthy*; producing health and growth: *a nourishing diet.*

- **Neglect** not the gift that is in thee, which was given thee by prophecy, with the laying on of the hands of the presbytery. Meditate upon these things; give thyself wholly to them; that thy profiting may appear to all. Take heed unto thyself, and unto the doctrine; continue in them: for in doing this thou shalt both save thyself, and them that hear thee. <u>1 Timothy 4:14-16</u>

- Sing unto the LORD, O ye saints of his, and give thanks at the remembrance of his holiness. For his anger *endureth but* a moment; in his favour *is* life: weeping may endure for a night, but joy *cometh* in the morning. And in my prosperity I said, I shall **never** be moved. <u>Psalms 30:4-6</u>

- If thou put the brethren in remembrance of these things, thou shalt be a good minister of Jesus Christ, **nourished** up in the words of faith and of good doctrine, whereunto thou hast attained. But refuse profane and old wives' fables, and exercise thyself *rather* unto godliness. For bodily exercise profiteth little: but godliness is profitable unto all things, having promise of the life that now is, and of that which is to come. This *is* a faithful saying and worthy of all acceptation. For therefore we both labour and suffer reproach, because we trust in the living God, who is the Saviour of all men, specially of those that believe. <u>1 Timothy 4:6-10</u>

Concentrate on the <u>needful</u> things, situation or moment.

O – Fifteen (15)

Obedience: an obeying; doing what one is told.

Offend: hurt the feelings of; make angry; displease; pain. Affect in an unpleasant or disagreeable way. Sin or do wrong.

Oppression: govern harshly; keep down unjustly or by cruelty: *The dictator oppressed the people*. Weigh down; lie heavily on; burden: A sense of trouble ahead oppressed her spirits. Cruel or unjust treatment; tyranny; persecution; despotism. Oppression of the poor can lead to revolution. They fought against oppression. A heavy, weary feeling of the body or mind; depression.

- If thou count me therefore a partner, receive him as myself. If he hath wronged thee, or oweth *thee* ought, put that on mine account; I Paul have written *it* with mine own hand, I will repay *it*: albeit I do not say to thee how thou owest unto me even thine own self besides. Yea, brother, let me have joy of thee in the Lord: refresh my bowels in the Lord. Having confidence in thy **obedience** I wrote unto thee, knowing that thou wilt also do more than I say. But withal prepare me also a lodging: for I trust that through your prayers I shall be given unto you. Philemon 1:17-22

- At the same time came the disciples unto Jesus, saying, Who is the greatest in the kingdom of heaven? And Jesus called a little child unto him, and set him in the midst of them, And said, Verily I say unto you, Except ye be converted, and become as little children, ye shall not enter into the kingdom of heaven. Whosoever therefore shall humble himself as this little child, the same is greatest in the kingdom of heaven. And whoso shall receive one such little child in my name receiveth me. But whoso shall **offend** one of these little ones which believe in me, it were better for him that a millstone were hanged about his neck, and *that* he were drowned in the depth of the sea. Matthew 18:1-6

- And thou shalt take no gift: for the gift blindeth the wise, and perverteth the words of the righteous. Also thou shalt not **oppress** a stranger: for ye know the heart of a stranger, seeing ye were strangers in the land of Egypt. Exodus 23:8-9

44

<u>Open</u> your heart and forget about the negative and forgive.

P - Sixteen (16)

Peace: freedom from strife of any kind; condition of quiet, order, and security: peace in the family. Freedom from war: *Work for world peace.* Agreement between contending parties to end war: *Sign the peace.*

Perfect: without defect; free from any flaw; faultless: a perfect spelling paper. Completely skilled; expert: *A perfect golfer.* Having all its parts; complete: *The set was perfect; nothing was missing or broken.* Exact; precise: *A perfect copy.* A perfect circle. Entire; total.

Pray: speak to God in worship; enter into spiritual communion with God; offer worship. Make earnest request to God or to any other object of worship: *Pray for help, pray for one's family.* Ask earnestly; implore.

- Thou wilt keep him in perfect **peace**, whose mind is stayed on thee: because he trusteth in thee. Trust ye in the LORD for ever: for in the LORD JEHOVAH is everlasting strength: For he bringeth down them that dwell on high; the lofty city, he layeth it low; he layeth it low, even to the ground; he bringeth it even to the dust. <u>Isaiah 26:3-5</u>

- The LORD will **perfect** that which concerneth me: thy mercy, O LORD, endureth for ever: forsake not the works of thine own hands. <u>Psalms 138:8</u>

- Now we exhort you, brethren, warn them that are unruly, comfort the feebleminded, support the weak, be patient toward all *men*. See that none render evil for evil unto any *man*; but ever follow that which is good, both among yourselves, and to all *men*. Rejoice evermore. **Pray** without ceasing. In every thing give thanks: for this is the will of God in Christ Jesus concerning you. <u>1 Thessalonians 5:14-18</u>

47

Be <u>patient</u> and trust God, through Jesus.

Q – Seventeen (17)

Quench: put an end to; stop: quench one's thirst. Drown out; out: *Water quenched the fire.* Cool suddenly by plunging into water or other liquid.

Quick: done, happening, or taking place in a very short time; fast and sudden; swift: *With a quick turn I avoided hitting the other car.* Begun and ended speedily. Coming soon; prompt; immediate; rapid.

Quietness: making or having little or no noise; almost silent; hushed: *Quiet footsteps, a quiet room.* Moving very little; still; calm: *A quiet river.*

- Stand therefore, having your lions girt about with truth, and having on the breastplate of righteousness. And your feet shod with the preparation of the gospel of peace; Above all, taking the shield of faith, wherewith ye shall be able to **quench** all the fiery darts of the wicked. And take the helmet of salvation, and the sword of the spirit, which is the word of God. <u>Ephesians 6:14-17</u>

- For the word of God is **quick** and powerful, and sharper than any two-edged sword, piercing even to the dividing asunder of souls and spirit, and of the joints and marrow, and is a discerner of the thoughts and intents of the hear. <u>Hebrews 4:12</u>

- For thus saith the Lord God, the Holy One of Israel; In returning and rest shall ye be saved; in **quietness** and in confidence shall be your strength: and ye would not. <u>Isaiah 30:15</u>

You have to know when to be <u>quiet</u>,
when to speak and when to share what
you're thinking, to people.

R – Eighteen (18)

Rest: the repose and refreshment offered by sleep; sleep: *A good night's rest*. Ease after work or effort; freedom from activity: *Allow an hour for rest*. Freedom from anything that tires, troubles, disturbs, or pains: respite. Absence of motion. Something to lean on.

Righteous: doing right; virtuous; behaving justly; a righteous person. Proper; just; right: righteous indignation. (**Right**: agreeing with what is good, just, or lawful: *She did the right thing when she told the truth*).

Run: go by moving the legs quickly; go faster than walking: *The cat ran away from the dog*. Go hurriedly; hasten: *Run for help*. Make a quick trip. Escape; flee. Go; move; keep going: *This train runs between Chicago and Los Angeles*. Sail or be driven.

- **Rest** in the LORD, and wait patiently for him: fret not thyself because of him who prospereth in his way, because of the man who bringeth wicked devices to pass. Cease from anger, and forsake wrath: fret not thyself in any wise to do evil. For evildoers shall be cut off: but those that wait upon the LORD, they shall inherit the earth. Proverbs 37:7-9

- The Lord is my shepherd; I shall not want. He maketh me to lie down in green pastures: he leadeth me beside the still waters. He restoreth my soul: he leadeth me in the paths of **righteousness** for his name sake. Yea though I walk through the valley of the shadow of death, I will fear no evil: for thou art with me; thy rod and thy staff they comfort me. Psalms 23:1-4

- But they that wait upon the LORD shall renew their strength; they shall mount up with wings as eagles; they shall **run**, and not be weary; and they shall walk, and not faint. Isaiah 40:31

For the best outcome pertaining to all things, you have to try and do what's __right__ and trust God.

S – Nineteen (19)

Saved: make safe from harm, danger, loss, etc.; rescue: *Save a drowning person.* Keep safe from harm, danger, hurt, loss, etc.; protect: save face. Lay aside; store up: *Save money.* Keep from spending or wasting: *We took the shortcut to save time.* Make less. Prevent: *Save work, save trouble save expense.*

Say: speak or pronounce; utter. Put into words; tell; declare: *Say what you think.* Recite; repeat: *Say one's prayers.* Take as an estimate; suppose. Express an opinion. Say words, talk.

Seek: try to find; look for: *We are seeking a new home.* Hunt; search for: *Seek something lost.* Try to get: *Seek advice.* Try; attempt: *Seek to make peace with one's enemies.* Go to. Make a search.

- But what saith it? The word is nigh thee, even in thy mouth, and in thy heart: that is, the word of faith, which we preach; That if thou shalt confess with thy mouth the Lord Jesus, and shalt believe in thine heart that God hath raised him from the dead, thou shalt be **saved**. For with the heart man believeth unto righteousness; and with the mouth confession is made unto salvation. For the scriptures saith, whosoever believeth on him shall not be ashamed. Romans 10:8-11

- And the apostles said unto the LORD, Increase our faith. And the LORD said, If ye had faith as a grain of mustard seed, ye might **say** unto this sycamine tree, Be thou plucked up by the root, and be thou planted in the sea; and it should obey you. Luke 17:5-6

- But **seek** ye first the kingdom of God, and his righteousness; and all these things shall be added unto you. Take therefore no thought for the morrow: for the morrow shall take thought for the things of itself. Sufficient unto the day is the evil thereof. Matthew 6:33-34

Saying and believing what you have **said** is key to faith... Be assured that you can change any situation by what you say, unless it's a curse, plague or test from God.

T – Twenty (20)

Take: lay hold of; grasp. Seize; capture. Accept: *Take a bet.* Take my advice get, receive. Win: *Take first prize.* Have; get: take a seat. Obtain from source; derive.

Taste: what is special about (something) to the sense organs in the mouth and on the tongue; flavor: *Sweet, sour, salt, and bitter are four important tastes.* The sense by which the flavor of things is perceived. A little bit; sample. A liking. Ability to perceive and enjoy what is beautiful and excellent.

Trust: firm belief in the honesty, truthfulness, justice, or power of a person or thing; faith: *Children put trust in their parents.* A person or thing trusted: *His family was his only trust.* Confident expectation or hope. Something managed for the benefit of another. Something committed to one's care. Obligation or responsibility imposed on one in whom confidence or authority is placed; being relied on.

- Therefore **take** no thought, saying, What shall we eat? Or, What shall we drink? Or, Wherewithal shall we be clothed? (For after all these things do the Gentiles seek) for your heavenly Father knoweth that ye have need of all these things. But seek ye first the kingdom of God, and his righteousness; and all these things shall be added unto you. Matthew 6:31-33

- Oh **taste** and see that the Lord is good: blessed is the man that trusteth in him. Psalms 34:8

- **Trust** in the LORD, and do good; so shalt thou dwell in the land, and verily thou shalt be fed. Psalm 37:3

*Keep **trying** you still have at least six (6) more ways. And if your trusting God, you have until eternity. He's a just and forgiving God, He doesn't judge but corrects you. He desires' that we all win, conquer and give Him the glory that's do unto Him.*

U – Twenty-one (21)

Unequal: not the same in amount, size, number, value, degree, rank, etc.: *Unequal sums of money.* Not balanced; not well matched. Not fair; one-sided: *An unequal contest.* Not enough; not adequate: *Strength unequal to the task.* Not regular; not even; variable.

Ungodly: not devout; not religious; impious. Wicked; sinful. very annoying; outrageous; shocking: *An ungodly noise, pay an ungodly price.*

Unity: a being united; oneness; singleness: *A circle has unity*; a random group of dots does not. Union of parts forming a complex whole. Concord: harmony: *Brothers and sisters should live together in unity.*

- Be ye not **unequally** yoked together with unbelievers: for what fellowship hath righteousness with unrighteousness? And what communion hath light with darkness? And what concord hath Christ with Beliah? Or what part hath he that believeth with an infidel? 2 Corinthians 6:14-15

- Blessed is the man that walketh not in the counsel of the **ungodly**, nor standeth in the way of sinners, nor sitteth in the seat of the scornful. But his delight is in the law of the Lord; and in his law doth he meditate day and night. And he shall be like a tree planted by the rivers of water, that bringeth forth his fruit in his season, his leaf also shall not wither, and whatsoever he doeth shall prosper. Psalms 1:1-3

- I therefore, the prisoner of the LORD, beseech you that ye walk worthy of the vocation wherewith ye are called, With all lowliness and meekness, with longsuffering, forbearing one another in love; Endeavouring to keep the **unity** of the Spirit in the bond of peace. Ephesians 4:1-3

- Behold, How Good and how pleasant it is for brethren to dwell together in **unity**! Psalms 133:1

Having an __unconditional__ mind set and doing something for someone else because it's correct or it's in your heart will help you to be stress free and full of peace.

V – Twenty-two (22)

Victory: defeat of an enemy or opponent; success in a contest. Victory, conquest, triumph mean success in a contest or struggle. Victory applies to success in any kind of contest or fight. Absolute control of the defeated. Triumph applies to a glorious victory or conquest.

Vigilant: keeping steadily on the alert; watchful; wide awake.

Vision: power of seeing; sense of sight: *She wore glasses to improve her vision.* Act or fact of seeing; sight. Power of perceiving by the imagination or by clear thinking. Something seen in the imagination, in a dream, in one's thoughts, etc.

- For this is the love of God, that we keep his commandments: and his commandments are not grievous. For whatsoever is born of God overcometh the world: and this is the **victory** that overcometh the world, even our faith. Who is he that overcometh the world, but he that believeth that Jesus is the Son of God. <u>1 John 5:3-5</u>

- Humble yourselves therefore under the mighty hand of God, that he may exalt you in due time: Casting all your care upon him; for he careth for you. Be sober, be **vigilant**: because your adversary the devil, as a roaring lion, walketh about, seeking whom he may devour. <u>1 Peter 5:6-8</u>

- Where there is no **vision**, the people perish: but he that keepeth the law, happy is he. <u>Proverbs 29:18</u>

**Victories** comes from trying and not giving up. If the Word of God says it shall happen, then it will.

W – Twenty-three (23)

Walk: go on foot. In walking, a person always has one foot on the ground. Roam. Go slowly. (of things) move or shake in a manner suggestive of walking. Conduct oneself in a particular manner; behave; live: *Walk in the ways of God.*

Wisdom: knowledge and good judgment based on experience; being wise. Wise conduct; wise words. Scholarly knowledge.

Worship: great honor and reverence paid to someone or something regarded as sacred: *The worship of God, idol worship, fire worship.* Religious ceremonies or services in which one expresses such honor and reverence. Great love and admiration; adoration: *Hero worship.* The worship of wealth and power.

- Then Jesus said unto them, Yet a little while is the light with you. Walk while ye have the light, lest darkness come upon you: for he that walketh in darkness knoweth not whither he goeth. While ye have light, believe in the light, that ye may be the children of light. These things spake Jesus, and departed and did hide himself from them. John 11:35-36

- Hear, Ye children, the instruction of a father, and attend to know understanding. For I give you good doctrine, forsake ye not my law. For I was my father's son tender and only beloved in the sight of my mother. He taught me also, and said unto me, Let thine heart retain my words: keep my commandments, and live. Get wisdom, get understanding: forget it not; neither decline from the words of my mouth. Forsake her not, and she shall preserve thee: love her, and she shall keep thee. Wisdom is the principal thing; therefore get wisdom: and with all thy getting get understanding. Proverbs 4:1-7

- The woman saith unto him, Sir, I perceive that thou art a prophet. Our fathers worshipped in this mountain; and ye say, that in Jerusalem is the place where men ought to worship. Jesus saith unto her, Woman, believe me, the hour cometh, when ye shall neither in this mountain, nor yet at Jerusalem, worship the Father. Ye worship ye know not what: we know what we worship: for salvation is of the Jews. But the hour cometh, and now is, when the true worshippers shall worship the Father in spirit and in truth: for the Father seeketh such to worship him. God is a Spirit: and they that worship him must worship him in spirit and in truth. John 4:19-24

*Concentrate and **work** towards doing what's correct (right) daily.*

X – Twenty-four (24)

Exceeding: very great; unusual. Exceedingly: *Very greatly*; extremely.

Excellent: of usually good quality; better than others; superior. **Excel**: be better than; do better than. Be better than others; do better than others.

Extol: praise highly; commend.

- For this cause I bow my knees unto the Father of our Lord Jesus Christ. Of whom the whole family in heaven and earth is named, That he would grant you, according to the riches of his glory, to be strengthened with might by his Spirit in the inner man; That Christ may dwell in your hearts by faith; that ye, being rooted and grounded in love, May be able to comprehend with all saints what is the breadth, and length, and depth and height; And to know the love of Christ, which passeth knowledge, that ye might be filled with all the fulness of God. Now unto him that is able to do **exceeding** abundantly above all that we can ask or think, according to the power that worketh in us (you).
Ephesians 3:14-20

- Unto you, O men, I call; and my voice is to the sons of man. O ye simple, understand wisdom: and, ye fools, be ye of an understanding heart. Hear; for I will speak of **excellent** things; and the opening of my lips shall be right things. For my mouth shall speak truth; and wickedness is an abomination to my lips. All the words of my mouth are in righteousness; there is nothing froward or perverse in them.
Proverbs 8:4-8

- *(A Psalm and Song at the dedication of the house of David.)* I will **extol** thee, O LORD; for thou hast lifted me up, and hast not made my foes to rejoice over me. Psalms 30:1

71

*If you're doing your best, can't no other person's **excellent** be better than yours regarding you, when you're doing your best.*

Y – Twenty-five (25)

<u>Yield</u>: produce; bear: *Land yields crops*; mines yield ore. Give in return; bring in: *And investment which yielded a large profit*. Give; grant. Bear produce; be productive. Give up; surrender: *The enemy yielded to our soldiers*.

<u>Yoke</u>: a wooden frame to fasten two work animals together. Pair fastened together by a yoke: *The plow was drawn by a yoke of oxen*. Any frame connecting two other parts: She carried two buckets on a yoke, one at each end. Part of a garment fitting the neck and shoulders closely. Something that joins or unites; bond; tie. Something that holds people in slavery or submission. Join, unite: *Be yoked in marriage*. Be joined or united.

<u>Young/Youth</u>: in the early part of life or growth; not old: a puppy is a young dog. Having the looks or qualities of youth or a young person. Of youth; early: one's young days. Not as old as another or the other. In an early age; not far advanced. Without much experience or practice.

- Let the people praise thee, O God; let all the people praise thee. O let all the people praise thee. O let the nations be glad and sing for joy: for thou shalt judge the people righteously and govern the nations upon earth. Selah. Let the people praise thee, O God; let all the people praise thee. Then shall the earth **yield** her increase; and God, even our own God, shall bless us. God shall bless us; and all the ends of the earth shall fear him. Psalms 67:3-7

- Come unto me, all ye that labour and are heavy laden, and I will give you rest. Take my **yoke** upon you, and learn of me; for I am meek and lowly in heart: and ye shall find rest unto your souls. For my yoke is easy, and my burden is light. Matthew 11:28-30

- For therefore we both labour and suffer reproach, because we trust in the living God, who is the Saviour of all men, specially of those that believe. These things command and teach. Let no man despise thy **youth**; but be thou an example of the believers in word, in conversation, in charity, in spirit, in faith, in purity. Till I come, give attendance to reading; to exhortation, to doctrine. 1 Timothy 4:10-13

74

Know when to say __yes__ and know when to say no. It's okay to say no especially when a particular situation doesn't agree with your spirit and God's Word.

Z - Twenty-six (26)

Zacchaeus: a very rich person in the bible who gave a lot. And was considered righteous and fair in the eyes of God.

Zacharias: the father of John the Baptist. Man mentioned as a martyr in the New Testament. Him and his wife Elizabeth were aged, but desired to have children. And because of their righteousness disposition, God gave them a child to raise, (allowed Elisabeth to become pregnant) with John the Baptist, who was the for-runner for Jesus.

Zealous: full of zeal; eager; earnest; enthusiastic: zealous efforts to clean up the house.

- And Jesus entered and passed through Jericho. And, behold, there was a man named **Zacchaeus**, which was the chief among the publicans, and he was rich. And he sought to see Jesus who he was; and could not for the press, because he was little of stature. And he ran before, and climbed up into a sycamore tree to see him: for he was to pass that way. And when Jesus came to the place, he looked up, and saw him, and said unto him, Zacchaeus, make haste, and come down; for to day I must abide at thy house. And he made haste, and came down, and received him joyfully. And when they saw it, they all murmured, saying, That he was gone to be guest with a man that is a sinner. And **Zacchaeus** stood, and said unto the LORD: Behold, LORD, the half of my goods I give to the poor; and if I have taken any thing from any man by false accusation, I restore him fourfold. And Jesus said unto him, This day is salvation come to this house, forsomuch as he also is a son of Abraham. For the Son of man is come to seek and to save that which was lost. Luke 19:1-10

- There was in the days of Herod, the king of Judaea, a certain priest named **Zacharias**, of the course of Abia; and his wife was of the daughter of Aaron and her names was Elisabeth. And they were both righteous before God, walking in all the commandments and ordinances of the Lord blameless. Luke 1:5-6

- Righteous art thou, O LORD, and upright are thy judgments. Thy testimonies that thou hast commanded are righteous and very faithful. My **zeal** hath consumed me, because mine enemies have forgotten thy words. Thy word is very pure: therefore thy servant loveth it. Psalms 119:137-140

*God is no respector of person's; if He did a miracle for **Zacchaeus** and **Zacharias** he will also perform one for you, us, all who ask.*

Brenda J. Mills is a public service retiree. She worked in the public school setting for more than thirty years in the capacity of a noon hour aide, secretary, certified K-8, all subjects teacher and as a McKinney Vento Homeless Liaison.

She has more than seventeen years of experience as a biblical youth teacher, annually supported Vacation Bible School for more than fifteen years, with five of those years as the director of VBS. And for more than seven years she worked with children in the Alphabet Soup Program, a neighborhood program that was granted and sponsored through a neighborhood Presbyterian Church.

This book (26) Ways (78) Reasons Don't Give Up, is *Brenda's* fourth authored book. **The Children's Bread, The Children's Bread (2)** and **The Children's Bread for Toddlers**, are previously written books by *Brenda* which are also spiritually minded related.

Brenda considers herself to be a creative writer which complements and goes along perfectly with her other skills, as a dressmaker, fabric re-constructor, home decorator, and artist.